ADA LOVELACE

Ada Lovelace
1815 – 1852

COMPUTER PROGRAMMER

Ada grew up in England during the Industrial Revolution, a time when scientists and artists gathered to discuss new inventions and creations. At one meeting, Ada met mathematician Charles Babbage, who had devised a mechanical adding machine. She was inspired and wanted to work with him! To prove herself capable, she translated an Italian article about his new machine into English and added her own notations on how it could be programmed. She imagined a general-purpose computer a century before anyone would build one. Ada's work is considered the first-ever computer program, which made her the first computer programmer.

IDA B. WELLS

JOURNALIST, ACTIVIST

Ida was born enslaved in Mississippi, but emancipation came to the South when she was still a child, and this meant she had the opportunity to get an education. She became most well known for her journalism—but even before she ran several papers and took a major stance against lynching, Ida had been fighting for justice. In 1884, seventy-one years before Rosa Parks refused to give up her seat on a bus in Montgomery, Alabama, Ida refused to leave her seat in the women's car on a train in Memphis, Tennessee.

Ida knew the power of words and knowledge, and she used her voice to stand up for what was right.

MARIE CURIE

Marie Curie
1867 – 1934

PHYSICIST, CHEMIST

When Marie was growing up in Poland, women weren't allowed to study in universities, so she had to learn in secret. Eventually, she studied at the University of Paris and earned two degrees, in physics and mathematics. In 1896, she began researching uranium salts and wanted to understand why they emitted a weird glow. She concluded that it was happening at the atomic level and called this radioactivity. Her husband, Pierre, joined her research and together they discovered two new elements: radium and polonium. Marie was the first person to be awarded Nobel Prizes in two different fields: Physics and Chemistry.

BESSIE COLEMAN

Bessie Coleman
1892–1926

PILOT

Bessie grew up in a small segregated town in Texas. In 1915, she moved to Chicago to live with her older brothers, who had returned from World War I. They told her about how women in France could fly planes, and Bessie knew that's what she wanted to do. She moved to France to go to aviation school, and in 1921, she became the first African American woman in the world to receive her pilot's license.

After returning home to the United States, Bessie flew for huge crowds. She was popular among both white and black Americans and stood up against segregation and discrimination whenever she could.

JOSEPHINE BAKER

SINGER, DANCER

The first time Josephine performed onstage, she made waves with her wild dancing. She stood out from the chorus line, and the other performers called her a scene stealer. But that was just Josephine's style.

Josephine's career took off when she went to Europe. During World War II, Josephine worked for the French Résistance, smuggling secret messages in her sheet music. When she performed in the United States, she fought for integrated audiences, and in 1963 she was the only woman to speak at the famous March on Washington. She was a brave woman who was so much more than just a performer.

FRIDA KAHLO

PAINTER

Frida had a difficult life but was able to channel her tragedy and pain into art. She learned to paint while bedridden, and with nothing else to look at, she painted herself. She painted not only what she saw but also what she felt. Her self-portraits, which she is most famous for, were a mix of exuberant, sad, colorful, and dark. She had a revolutionary spirit and incorporated her social and political opinions into her work, as well as her passion for indigenous Mexican culture. Frida celebrated her country's heritage and captured the fears and struggles of its people in her paintings.

GYO FUJIKAWA

Gyo Fujikawa

1908–1998

ILLUSTRATOR

Gyo showed a love for art early in life, and her drive and skill took her far. She studied traditional brush painting in Japan and later worked for Walt Disney Productions. Soon her work got her noticed by a book publisher, and she was hired to illustrate a new edition of Robert Louis Stevenson's *A Child's Garden of Verses*. She later published the very popular books *Babies* and *Baby Animals* along with over forty more titles. Gyo took special care in her work to consider what a child might enjoy and to celebrate diversity with her sweet, round-cheeked characters of many different ethnicities.

ROSA PARKS

Rosa Parks
1913 - 2005

ACTIVIST, WRITER

Rosa grew up in the South, where rules for riding the bus were particularly harsh for black people. In December 1955, after a long shift at work, Rosa waited for a bus with empty seats, and finally got one. But before long, she was asked to move. She refused—and was arrested. Rosa's protest got a lot of attention and led to the Montgomery Bus Boycott, a key event of the Civil Rights Movement. In 1956, the bus system was integrated! But there was still a long way to go toward equality, so Rosa continued to fight for civil rights throughout her life.

HEDY LAMARR

ACTRESS, INVENTOR

Hedy was always curious and creative, and she loved to learn about how things worked. As a teenager, she began to act in films in her native Austria. Before World War II, Hedy escaped to Hollywood and starred in big films like *Samson and Delilah*. She always worked on her own projects and inventions. During the war she had an idea for a communications system that could transmit codes and make them unbreakable. Although the invention was not used then, it was the basis for the technology behind wireless signals used in GPS, Bluetooth, and Wi-Fi.

SISTER ROSETTA THARPE

Sister Rosetta Tharpe
1915–1973

MUSICIAN

By the age of six, Rosetta was already performing music in front of a crowd. She traveled the country with her mother, a gospel singer and preacher, and was praised for her singing and guitar skills. In 1938, Rosetta signed a landmark deal with Decca Records. She was their first gospel artist, and she bridged the worlds of religious and secular music. She helped shape the rock-and-roll genre with her hit song "Rock Me" and her pioneering use of the newly electrified guitar. Rosetta was a trailblazer and is celebrated as the Godmother of Rock and Roll.

KATHERINE JOHNSON

NASA MATHEMATICIAN

As a child, Katherine skipped seven grades and graduated ahead of her older siblings. As a young woman, she was a math teacher before she pursued a career as a research mathematician.

Katherine's first assignment at NASA's Langley Research Center, which had recently opened a lab that hired African American mathematicians, was to the flight research division. NASA's big goal at the time was to get a man on the moon. Katherine helped make it happen by calculating the flight path. She continued computing at NASA until her retirement in 1986, and her work influenced every major space program up to that point.

SISTER CORITA KENT

Sister Corita Kent
1918–1986

ARTIST, EDUCATOR

Like most young artists, Frances Kent loved to draw, read, and make things. From a young age she also knew she wanted to become a nun. At eighteen she entered the Roman Catholic religious order and became known as Sister Mary Corita or simply Corita. At Immaculate Heart College in Los Angeles, Corita studied art and later began teaching. In her early days, Corita focused mainly on religious subject matter. Inspired by the artist Andy Warhol's work, she began making Pop Art, using mass-market imagery as a way to reach people with messages of love and compassion.

MAYA ANGELOU

Maya Angelou
1928–2014

POET, ACTIVIST

Long before Maya was a writer and poet, she was a little girl in Stamps, Arkansas, trying to find her voice. She experienced abuse at a young age, and the trauma from it was powerful enough to convince her to stop speaking. For five years Maya didn't utter a word. But during those years, she read. A lot. Encouraged by a mentor, Maya spoke again. Maya went on to write the bestselling *I Know Why the Caged Bird Sings*, a lyrical and poetic telling of her childhood. In 1992, she became the first woman to write and recite a poem for the presidential inauguration, which brought her poetry into the mainstream again.

TONI MORRISON

Toni Morrison
1931–2019

WRITER

Growing up, Toni was influenced by her African American heritage and its strong tradition of storytelling. As an adult, she worked as a college professor and as an editor at a big publisher, where she championed writers of color. At thirty-nine she published her first novel, *The Bluest Eye,* and in 1993 she became the first black woman to win the Nobel Prize in Literature. Toni used her stories to address the African American experience and reflect the histories of America, often with magic, myth, and fantasy woven in. Her love for storytelling helped change American literature forever.

RAVEN WILKINSON

Raven Wilkinson
1935 – 2018

BALLERINA

Raven's love for dance began at age five, when her mother took her to a performance by the Ballet Russe de Monte Carlo. In 1955, Raven was accepted into that company despite being warned by friends that they would never take her because she was black. Her talent was undeniable, though, and she made history by becoming their first full-time African American dancer.

Raven danced until she was fifty. Her strength and grace led the way for dancers such as Misty Copeland to take on the role of principal dancer at the American Ballet Theatre and defy long-standing beauty and body standards for ballerinas.

WANGARI MAATHAI

Wangari Maathai
1940–2011

ENVIRONMENTALIST, ACTIVIST

Wangari was born in Kenya and hails from a clan known for its leadership. She developed a love for science and became the first woman in east or central Africa to earn a doctorate. As part of the National Council of Women of Kenya, Wangari had the idea that women throughout the country should plant trees to conserve the environment and improve their quality of life. She expanded this idea into the Green Belt Movement, which led to the planting of twenty million trees. Wangari was also a member of the Parliament of Kenya, advocating for human rights and women's rights. In 2004, Wangari received the Nobel Peace Prize.

ANGELA DAVIS

ACTIVIST, SCHOLAR

Angela grew up in racially segregated Birmingham, Alabama, a city at the center of the fight for civil rights. By the time she was a teenager, Angela was already actively involved in the movement. Some of her major passions were fighting for prison reform and against police brutality. She was labeled a troublemaker and was put on the FBI's most wanted list. When she was let go from her teaching job, she fired back with a lawsuit. She was put in prison for conspiracy charges, but she was acquitted sixteen months later. Angela is largely considered a symbol for fighting back against systems of oppression.

ZAHA HADID

ARCHITECT

Even as a child, Zaha had impeccable taste, and her mother let her design rooms in their home. At eleven years old, Zaha knew she wanted to design buildings. In architecture school she pushed the boundaries of design and was inspired to re-envision abstract paintings as buildings. She opened her own architecture firm in 1979 and became known for her dynamic forms, using curving shapes that flowed like water. She was the first woman to receive the Pritzker Architecture Prize—the field's most prestigious award. At the time of her death in 2016, she was considered one of the world's greatest architects.

RUBY BRIDGES

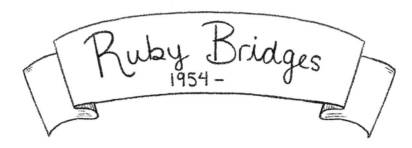

ACTIVIST

Ruby made history in 1960, when at the age of six she became the first black student to attend an all-white school in New Orleans. Many people did not support deseg-regation, but Ruby's mother knew her daughter would get a better education at this school. On Ruby's first day, protestors surrounded the school. She had to be escorted in by her mother and US marshals. White parents pulled their kids from classes, and many of the teachers refused to teach a black child. During the fight for civil rights, Ruby was a symbol for the vulnerability that all black Americans faced.

GWEN IFILL

Gwen Ifill
1955–2016

JOURNALIST

When Gwen was growing up, her family watched the television news together every evening. Gwen's interest in the way the world worked grew from there. After college, Gwen moved her way up from small newspapers to prestigious publications such as the *Washington Post* and the *New York Times* and then transitioned into television, landing a job at PBS. In 2013, Gwen and her colleague Judy Woodruff were hired as anchors of *NewsHour*, making them the first all-female network news team, and Gwen the first African American female anchor of a network news program. A trailblazer in her field, Gwen was a true professional, full of integrity and fairness.

The first
African American
woman astronaut

DR. MAE JEMISON

Dr. Mae Jemison
1956 –

ENGINEER, PHYSICIAN, ASTRONAUT

As a child, Mae loved to read books about science and astronomy. She knew she wanted to become a scientist. She also wanted to help people, so after graduating from college, she decided to become a doctor.

Mae had always imagined herself in space but was hesitant to pursue that dream. Seeing the actress Nichelle Nichols play Lieutenant Uhura in the TV show *Star Trek* inspired her to apply to the space program. In 1987, Mae became the first black woman in the astronaut training program, and a few years later she flew into orbit— as the first African American woman in space.

SOJOURNER TRUTH

Sojourner Truth
Circa 1797–1883

ABOLITIONIST, WOMEN'S RIGHTS ADVOCATE

Before Sojourner was the well-known preacher who traveled the country sharing her messages for women's rights and the abolition of slavery, she was an enslaved woman named Isabella Baumfree. She escaped slavery with her infant daughter but had to wait years and win a court case before she was reunited with her son. In 1851, she gave a speech advocating on behalf of black women who faced the double discrimination of racism and sexism. The speech is known by its most famous refrain: "Ain't I a Woman?"

She was an agitator and a fierce activist for equality.